AVALANCHES

MICHAEL WOODS
AND MARY B. WOODS

LERNER PUBLICATIONS COMPANY
MINNEAPOLIS

To Mark Woods

Editor's note: Determining the exact death toll following disasters is often difficult—if not impossible—especially in the case of disasters that took place long ago. The authors and the editors in this series have used their best judgment in determining which figures to include.

Lerner Publications Company
A division of Lerner Publishing Group
241 First Avenue North
Minneapolis, MN 55401 U.S.A.

Website address: www.lernerbooks.com

Library of Congress Cataloging-in-Publication Data

Woods, Michael, 1946–
    Avalanches / by Michael Woods and Mary B. Woods.
        p.   cm. — (Disasters up close)
    Includes bibliographical references and index.
    ISBN-13: 978-0-8225-6577-2 (lib. bdg. : alk. paper)
    ISBN-10: 0-8225-6577-3 (lib. bdg. : alk. paper)
    1. Avalanches—Juvenile literature.   I. Woods, Mary B. (Mary Boyle), 1946– II. Title.
QC929.A8W66   2007
363.34'9—dc22
                                                            2006020205

Manufactured in the United States of America
1 2 3 4 5 6 – DP – 12 11 10 09 08 07

Contents

Introduction

IT WAS A LATE SUMMER NIGHT ON SEPTEMBER 20, 2002. DMITRY PODALYAKIN WAS WITH FRIENDS AT A CAFÉ IN THE CAUCASUS MOUNTAINS OF NORTH OSSETIA, RUSSIA. MANY VISITORS HAD COME TO THIS BEAUTIFUL AREA TO CAMP AND HIKE FOR THE WEEKEND. EVERYONE WAS EXCITED THAT ONE OF RUSSIA'S HOTTEST MOVIE STARS, SERGEI BODROV JR., WAS IN THE AREA TO SHOOT A NEW FILM.

Suddenly, a tremendous roaring noise made Podalyakin and his friends jump to their feet. They looked up and saw that a huge chunk of ice had broken off from the side of nearby Mount Dzhimara. The mountain was 15,700 feet (4,785 meters) high and covered with ice and snow year-round.

The ice shattered as it crashed down the mountainside. It looked like a gigantic ocean wave. The avalanche moved at more than 60 miles (100 kilometers) per hour. As the ice whooshed along, it scooped up dirt, rocks, and trees. It smashed everything in its path.

Podalyakin and his friends ran for their lives. "When we came back, we saw that some of the cabins were covered by the mass [of ice]," he remembered. "There were cries of 'Save us!' but we could do nothing except stand there. Soon the cries stopped."

An avalanche had buried many people alive. In this avalanche, the ice was nearly 500 feet (152 m) thick and almost 1,000 feet (305 m) wide. It weighed 20 million tons (18 million metric tons). It tumbled 20 miles (33 km) down the mountain and onto the surrounding countryside. On its way, the

Melting ice from the North Ossetia avalanche caused mudslides. Emergency workers struggled to find missing people in the mud and ice.

avalanche snapped trees as though they were toothpicks. It knocked down power lines and smashed houses. One village was buried in ice almost 400 feet (123 m) deep.

"You couldn't do anything," said one eyewitness. "It was all over in a moment." Ruslan Mutsuyev, an emergency worker, said many people were sleeping in their houses, tents, or campers when the avalanche hit. He added, "Most people would have been taken completely by surprise."

The avalanche caused great destruction. It killed at least 125 people, including Sergei Bodrov.

"It sounded like a train was coming. But there are no trains here."

—Dmitry Podalyakin, on the 2002 avalanche in North Ossetia, Russia

A 20-mile-long (33 km) landslide of ice, mud, and rock blocked roads after the avalanche in North Ossetia.

What Are Avalanches?

AN AVALANCHE IS A MASS OF SNOW OR ICE THAT BREAKS LOOSE FROM THE SIDE OF A MOUNTAIN. IT TUMBLES DOWN WITH GREAT SPEED AND POWER. THE SNOW AND ICE CAN BURY OR DESTROY EVERYTHING IN ITS PATH.

The word *avalanche* comes from a French word for descent (falling down). *Avalanche* can refer to falling snow, ice, rocks, or soil. However, falling rocks and soil are typically known as landslides.

THE WHITE DEATH

Avalanches have been called the White Death. They can easily kill a skier or snowmobiler. They can also bury entire villages and cause terrible disasters. Disasters are events that harm a large number of people.

In 1999 a giant avalanche buried two villages in France in snow 15 feet (4.6 m) deep. "When I got there, I couldn't believe my eyes," said Mike Cooper, an eyewitness. "Nothing in the path of the avalanche had withstood its force. More than a dozen houses had disappeared." That avalanche killed 12 people. The White Death has taken the lives of many more people throughout history. During World War I (1914–1918), avalanches in Europe killed 60,000 soldiers.

Avalanches are so deadly because they often happen with no warning. One minute a mountainside is a picture-perfect scene of sparkling snow. The next minute, a wall of snow is thundering down.

SNOW ON THE RUN

Avalanches do not fall or tumble. They *run*. That's the correct word to describe an avalanche's downward movement.

A snow and ice avalanche
runs down a mountainside
in Antarctica.

BIG AND FAST

The average avalanche involves snow 3 feet (0.9 m) deep and about 150 feet (46 m) wide. It falls down 400 feet (122 m) at a speed of about 50 miles (80 km) per hour.

Big avalanches may have enough snow to cover 20 football fields 10 feet (3 m) deep. They can be more than 1 mile (1.6 km) wide and travel for 5 miles (8 km). The snow can move at more than 80 miles (129 km) per hour. That's faster than a speeding car on the highway. One avalanche in Japan roared down at a speed of 245 miles (394 km) per hour.

SLAB, LOOSE SNOW, POWDER, AND ICE AVALANCHES

Avalanches can be divided into several main categories. Slab avalanches are the most common and most deadly. They are chunks of snow that break off and slide down a slope. A chunk can be more than 10 feet (3 m) thick and bigger than several football fields. As it tumbles down, the snow may collect rocks, soil, and trees that help smash everything in its path.

Slab avalanches can involve dry or wet snow. Dry slab avalanches move faster than any other kind. They are extremely dangerous.

Wet slab avalanches move more slowly and are easier to predict. They usually happen in spring, when snow starts to melt. Melting snow doesn't stick to other snow very well. Heavy layers of snow can break off and slip.

INSIDE A WASHING MACHINE

Bruce Tremper remembers being caught in an avalanche. He directs the Forest Service Utah Avalanche Center.

"You rocket down the slope and pick up speed very quickly," he said. "At five seconds you're going 40 miles [64 km] per hour. At ten seconds, you're going 80 [129 km]. You tumble over and over like being in a giant washing machine. It rips away your hat and mittens. Your own boots are kicking you in the back of the head. The mixture of air and snow instantly forms a plug of ice in your mouth."

In a slab avalanche, a huge amount of snow can break off and slide. The line where the slab broke off is visible farther up the mountainside.

Loose snow avalanches are the other main type of avalanche. These happen when a small amount of snow releases from a point. The snow spreads out and collects more snow as it runs. Loose snow avalanches can be destructive if they involve heavy, wet snow.

Sometimes a third kind of avalanche happens. Airborne avalanches, or powder avalanches, contain powdery snow that shoots down a mountain through the air. These avalanches can move at 200 miles (322 km) per hour. Pressure builds up in front of the avalanche and creates a powerful blast of air. It can sweep away people, animals, trees, and buildings.

Ice avalanches happen when blocks of ice break off from glaciers. Blocks can be bigger than a football field. Occasionally, when these avalanches happen near towns, they can cause disasters.

Powder avalanches, like this 2005 avalanche in France, can have devastating effects.

A GROWING THREAT

In an average year, about one million avalanches happen throughout the world. They kill as many as two hundred people and injure several thousand others. In the United States, around 100,000 avalanches occur each year. About twenty people are killed, and many more are injured.

These disasters may get worse. More people are enjoying winter sports and building houses in avalanche country. More people in these areas means more lives that future avalanches will threaten.

Building more houses in avalanche zones also means that future avalanches could cause more damage. Avalanches cause billions of dollars in damage each year. They smash buildings, roads, railroads, and bridges. In addition, avalanches kill animals and destroy thousands of trees.

A skier is airborne on Mount Currie in British Columbia, Canada. Avalanches are a serious danger for mountain skiers.

"It's like having the **rug pulled out from underneath you.**
You fall down and get mixed up. You cannot stand **up, your head gets buried.**
Your skis come off and **you kick and swim and kick and fight** to stay on the surface."

—Peter Schaerer, founder of the Canadian Avalanche Association, who has been caught in two avalanches

218 B.C.
HANNIBAL CROSSING THE ALPS

Hannibal directed his army, including a caravan of elephants, as they crossed the Alps in Europe.

In the spring of 218 B.C., Hannibal was getting nervous. He was the leader of Carthage, an ancient city in northern Africa. The Carthaginians owned rich silver mines in southern Spain. The Romans had gold mines in northern Spain, and Hannibal feared the Romans would take over his silver mines. So he decided to attack Rome.

Hannibal left Spain with an army of 90,000 foot soldiers, 12,000

The army had to cross the Alps, Europe's greatest mountain range, to reach Rome. Hannibal knew the mountains would be a problem.

When the army got through the French Alps, Hannibal told his soldiers that the worst was over. **"My men,"** he said, **"you are at this moment passing the protective barrier of Italy . . . you are walking over the very walls of Rome. [From now on] all will be easy**

But Hannibal did not realize what enemy waited ahead in the Italian Alps. It was not the Roman army. It was the White Death—avalanches.

The steep mountainsides were coated with heavy snow. As Hannibal's elephants walked, their footsteps shook the ground. The horses' and soldiers' footsteps also made the ground move.

Soon the movement caused great avalanches. Walls of snow smacked into Hannibal's soldiers. Avalanches buried some soldiers and horses alive. Silius Italicus, an ancient writer, reported that **"Snow falling rapidly from the high [peaks] engulfs the living."** Others were swept off the mountainsides and died when they smashed onto rocks below.

Avalanches hurt Hannibal's army in other ways too. When avalanches blocked the route, the army had to spend days clearing a path or taking a longer detour. During these delays, the men

"Detached snow drags the men into the abyss."

—Silius Italicus, on the 218 B.C. avalanche in the Italian Alps

suffered terribly in the cold. Most of them had never even *seen* snow. They were from northern Africa, where the weather usually is warm and sunny. Some froze to death. The elephants and horses suffered too. Food ran low, and the animals went hungry.

About 18,000 soldiers, two thousand horses, and several elephants died while crossing the Alps. Avalanches and the cold killed about half of them.

Hannibal made it out of the mountains and recruited more troops into his army. He defeated the Romans in several battles but was not successful in the end.

Many of Hannibal's soldiers were killed by avalanches before ever battling the Roman army.

What Causes Avalanches?

AVALANCHES HAVE TWO MAIN INGREDIENTS: STEEP MOUNTAINSIDES AND A COVERING OF ICE OR SNOW. MUCH OF THE TIME, HOWEVER, THE SNOW ON MOUNTAINS STAYS PUT. IT MAY STACK UP 20 FEET (6.1 M) ON A STEEP SLOPE. BUT IT STICKS TO THE MOUNTAINSIDE LIKE GLUE.

Stable snow or ice does not slip. For an avalanche to occur, something must make the snow and ice unstable.

AVALANCHE WEATHER

Snow can become unstable after a fresh snowfall. New snow may not stick firmly to the surface of snow already on a mountain. It also can add weight to the existing snow. This weight can set off an avalanche. Usually a storm must drop at least 6 inches (15 centimeters) of new snow to set off an avalanche.

If the new snow is wet, it is especially likely to cause an avalanche. Wet snow falls at warmer temperatures. It is very heavy. Water also makes the bottom layer of wet snow slippery, like water spilled on a floor. Slippery snow slides easily down a mountain.

THE AVALANCHE BEAST

What "flies without wings, strikes without hand, and sees without eyes"? To people who lived in the Alps long ago, it was *das Lauitier*. In German that means "the Avalanche-Beast."

FRESH FROZEN AVALANCHES

Changes in temperature can also lead to avalanches. Warm weather during the day melts the surface of the snow. The melted snow then freezes into ice when the temperature drops at night. The next day, a heavy snowfall might fall on top of that slippery, icy surface. The layer of new snow will be unstable.

14

ANATOMY OF A SLAB AVALANCHE

1 **starting zone:** the top portion of an avalanche path, where unstable snow breaks loose

2 **crown face:** the top boundary of a slab avalanche

3 **flanks:** the side boundaries of a slab avalanche

4 **bed surface:** the surface on which the avalanche slides

5 **stauchwall:** the lower boundary of the slab that breaks loose

6 **track:** the path between the starting zone and the runout zone

7 **runout zone:** the area where the avalanche stops

These temperature flip-flops, followed by new snow, may happen several times during the winter. They can leave the snow on a mountain looking like a layered cake. Some of those layers may become unstable enough to slip.

THE SNOWFLAKE FACTOR

Have you heard the saying "No two snowflakes are alike"? A single snowstorm may contain many trillions of snowflakes. Each one is slightly different.

Snowflakes are made from different kinds of snow crystals. Crystals are solid materials that have a pattern of flat surfaces. The pattern in snow crystals depends on the temperature at which moisture in the air changes into snow. The amount of moisture in the air also affects the pattern.

Snow crystals determine the shape of a snowflake. And the shape affects how stable the layers of snow are. Snowflakes made from crystals with many points are the most stable. Try linking the fingers of one hand with those of the other. The points on snow crystals lock together in almost the same way. They form layers of snow that are firmly packed and stable.

Snow crystals without points can slide and roll over one another. They make unstable layers of snow that can slide down in an avalanche.

SNOWFLAKE BENTLEY

Wilson Alwyn Bentley (1865–1931) took more than five thousand photographs of snowflakes through a microscope. He became known as Snowflake Bentley. His pictures showed that no two snowflakes are alike.

"Every crystal was a masterpiece of design and no one design was ever repeated," he said. "When a snowflake melted, that design was forever lost. Just that much beauty was gone, without leaving any record behind."

16

A 1999 avalanche destroyed this small village in France's Chamonix Valley, a popular skiing destination.

"My feet were cemented into the snow and I was on my knees. I really did think I was going to die."

—Maddie Sidani, who was caught in an avalanche in France in 1999

DANGEROUS SUGAR SNOW

An avalanche in March may happen because of snow that fell in November. That's because an especially dangerous kind of snow often falls early in the winter. It is coarse and grainy. This kind of snow is called depth hoar, or sugar snow. All the other layers of snow pile up on top of it during the winter.

Have you ever slipped on a sandy floor or tried to walk on marbles? Depth hoar has the same effect. It is an unstable base for the layers on top of it. The slightest disruption may trigger an avalanche.

WHO CAUSES AVALANCHES?

It takes only a tiny movement to make unstable snow rumble down and cause a disaster. Sometimes that movement comes from natural events, such as the weight of new snow or strong winds that form huge snowdrifts.

People, however, cause most avalanches. When people ski, snowboard, snowmobile, or hike over unstable snow, they cause small movements in the surface. Those movements travel down into the snow. They may cause unstable layers of snow to slip.

Sometimes people cause avalanches on purpose. Have you ever felt noise from a parade or stereo speaker vibrate in your chest? Extremely loud noises, such as an explosion, can cause the same vibrations in snow. Safety workers in some mountains set off explosions to make unstable snow slip before anyone can get hurt.

DID YOU KNOW?

In some countries, when dangerous piles of snow build up on a mountain, park rangers take special measures to prevent avalanches. They shoot into the snow with cannons when nobody is skiing *(right)*. The cannonballs break up slabs of snow that could tumble down onto people in killer avalanches. Rangers call it shooting the slopes.

This avalanche in Utah's Big Cottonwood Canyon was intentionally triggered. It was the first avalanche in 50 years to cross the road. Only the bottom fifth of the avalanche is visible in this photo.

March 1, 1910
WELLINGTON, WASHINGTON

The 1910 avalanche tore down telephone lines and covered buildings in Wellington.

In the early twentieth century, deep snows in the Cascade Mountains of Washington State nearly covered up the houses. In Wellington snow reached above the windows. No daylight could get in, so people had to keep the lights on all day.

The winter of 1910 was unusually harsh. One snowfall at the end of February was so deep that two Great Northern Railway trains got stuck on the tracks in Wellington. Snow fell for days. The trains sat below a steep mountain that was covered with 20 feet (6.1 m) of snow.

On March 1, a thunderstorm roared in with heavy rain and wind. Hundreds of feet above the railroad tracks, the rain and thunder caused a block of snow to break off the mountain. The block was 14 feet (4.3 m) deep, 2,000 feet (610 m) wide, and 2,100 feet (640 m) long. It smashed into the train and carried it down into the canyon below.

Charles Andrews, a railroad worker,

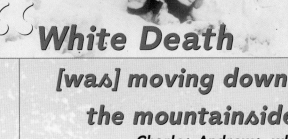

Pieces of two Great Northern Railway trains were scattered in the snow.

"White Death [was] moving down the mountainside above the trains."

—Charles Andrews, who witnessed the 1910 Wellington avalanche

saw the avalanche. He remembered it **"exploding, roaring, rumbling, grinding, snapping—[like] the crashing of ten thousand freight trains. It . . . picked up [train] cars and equipment as though they were . . . toys, and swallowing them up, disappeared like a white . . . monster into the ravine below."**

One train passenger remembered being awakened by the storm. **"Lightning flashes were vivid and a tearing wind was howling down the canyon. Suddenly there was a dull roar, and the sleeping men and women felt the passenger coaches lifted and [carried] along."**

A conductor in one of the train cars was asleep. He woke up when the avalanche started rolling the train over and over. He hit the roof, then the floor, then the roof—several times until the train car hit a large tree and broke apart.

The train cars tumbled for almost 1,000 feet (305 m). Rocks and trees inside the avalanche bashed the cars and tore some apart. When the avalanche finally stopped, it left the train covered in almost 40 feet (12 m) of snow.

It was the worst avalanche disaster in U.S. history. Ninety-six people were killed. Soon people wanted to forget it had happened. So they changed the name of the little town of Wellington to Tye.

Avalanche Country

AVALANCHES CAN HAPPEN ON ALMOST ANY STEEP, SNOWY MOUNTAIN. IN THE UNITED STATES, NEARLY ALL HAPPEN IN THE WEST. THE ROCKY MOUNTAIN STATES, WHICH INCLUDE COLORADO, IDAHO, MONTANA, NEVADA, UTAH, AND WYOMING, HAVE THE MOST AVALANCHES. OTHER DANGER ZONES INCLUDE MOUNTAINOUS AREAS IN WASHINGTON STATE, OREGON, CALIFORNIA, AND ALASKA.

An avalanche raced down the Swiss Alps in February 1999.

Some avalanches do occur in the mountains of New England in the eastern United States. Mountains in the West, however, are steeper. They also are higher and covered with snow longer.

Worldwide, most avalanches happen in the Alps. This great snowcapped mountain range stretches through Europe from France to Austria. Thousands of people live in villages that lie in Alpine avalanche zones. The Alps also are a popular spot for skiing and other winter sports that attract many visitors. Austria, Switzerland, France, and Italy have the most avalanches of the Alpine countries.

SLOWPOKE SLIDE
The world's slowest known avalanche happened on April 12, 1969, near Anchorage, Alaska. As people watched in amazement, a wall of snow about 30 feet (9 m) deep slid down at about 2 miles (3.2 km) per hour. A person can easily walk faster than that. The slow-motion avalanche destroyed a ski lift. It stopped just inches (centimeters) away from the ticket booth for the lift.

Avalanches occur in other parts of the world too, such as Norway and Sweden. They strike in the Canadian provinces of Alberta and British Columbia. And avalanches have caused huge disasters in Asia's Himalaya mountains and the Andes mountain range of South America.

WHEN AND WHO

Under the right conditions, avalanches can happen in any month of the year. But most avalanches happen in the winter. The snow is deepest then and most likely to slide. Snow sports also attract more people to the mountains in winter—more people who can trigger avalanches or be affected by them.

Most people caught in avalanches are in the mountains to have fun. They are skiing, snowboarding, snowmobiling, hiking, or mountain climbing. However, avalanches can trap anyone who happens to be in the way. Avalanche victims can be people who live in mountain villages, train passengers, or people driving in cars.

SOUND FISHY?

In 2002 an avalanche in Norway smashed into a fish farm. It killed 45,000 salmon. Fish farms have ponds in which farmers raise large numbers of fish. The avalanche filled the ponds with snow and buried the fish.

"**There's no one out there to save you** in an avalanche. **If you have to send for help, you're sending for a body recovery.**"

—Bruce Tremper, head of avalanche safety for the 2002 Winter Olympics in Salt Lake City, Utah

DISASTER ZONES

Avalanches can happen wherever snow and ice pile up on steep slopes. This map shows where some of the world's major avalanches have occurred. The boxed information describes especially destructive avalanches.

Galtur,
Austria
1999

ASIA

Tyrol area of the Alps
1915–1918 (60,000 deaths)

North Ossetia, Russia
2002 (at least 125 deaths)

Chamonix,
France
1999

EUROPE

Kashmir, India
1995 (more than 200 deaths)
2005 (at least 278 deaths)

Blons, Austria 1954

Salang, Afghanistan 1997

Vals, Switzerland
1951 (240 deaths)

Katmandu, Nepal 1995

AFRICA

AUSTRALIA

Chilkoot Pass, Alaska 1898

NORTH AMERICA

Wellington, Washington
1910 (96 deaths)

Ranrahirca, Peru
1962 (4,000 deaths)

SOUTH AMERICA

Yungay, Peru
1970 (18,000 deaths)

Chungar, Peru 1971

January 11, 1954
BLONS, AUSTRIA

People searched for survivors among the snow and rubble after the 1954 Blons avalanche.

Albert Dunser's parents warned him not to leave the house. A blizzard (heavy snowstorm) was raging outside. The mountain near their home in Blons, Austria, had more than 10 feet (3 m) of snow on it. Everyone was worried about an avalanche.

"I am going," Dunser said. Pirmin Schafer, a neighbor, was outside and saw Albert leave.

"You are crazy," Schafer said.

"Maybe not as crazy as you are to stay in your house," Dunser replied.

He meant that Schafer could be struck by an avalanche.

"Come, come, Albert," Schafer said. *"We are one hundred per cent safe here."* It was 9:36 A.M. on January 11, 1954. At that moment, Dunser and Schafer heard *"a crashing, swishing, roaring [noise]."*

They looked up and saw a neighbor's house flying toward them. Schafer ran into his house. But *"Albert stood [frozen with fear],"* author Joseph Wechsberg wrote in his account of the disaster. *"He couldn't move. He couldn't scream. . . . He just stood there."* The next instant, a steel wire flying through the air caught Dunser's coat. It carried him 800 feet (244 m) and dropped him in a snowbank, unharmed.

Other people in Blons were not so lucky. A wall of snow had broken loose from a nearby mountain and tumbled down. It destroyed Dunser's and Schafer's houses. Everyone inside died. Dozens of people in the village were killed or buried under 10 feet (3 m) of snow. And more snow kept falling.

The morning's avalanche didn't touch the home of "Mother" Dobler. Around 6:30 P.M., the 77-year-old was sitting in front of her wood-burning stove. The next thing she remembered was waking up and thinking, *"I am lying in my grave."* Her legs were stuck in a wall of ice. Her back was burning from red-hot chunks of wood spilled from the stove.

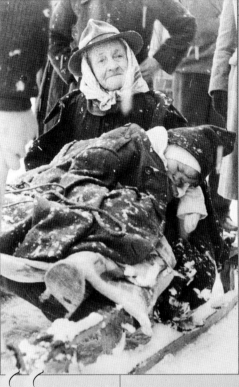

A grandmother and baby were rescued from their snow-crushed house in Blons.

Another avalanche had struck Blons. A 1,300-foot-long (396 m) block of snow bore down the mountain at 220 miles (354 km) per hour.

[I was] too weak to live and too tired to die.

—"Mother" Dobler, who survived 17 hours under the snow before being rescued in the 1954 Blons avalanche

In just 30 seconds, it buried forty people. Sixteen of them had been rescued from the first avalanche. They were some of the only people ever buried in two major avalanches in one day.

Rescuers went to work again. About 115 of Blons's 367 residents were buried in the avalanches. At least 55 of them died, and dozens were injured. One-third of the village's houses were destroyed. Mother Dobler was buried in the snow for 17 hours. She was rescued without serious injury.

Measuring Avalanches

MEASURING THE RISK OF AN AVALANCHE CAN TELL PEOPLE WHEN SKI SLOPES ARE SAFE TO USE AND WHEN THEY ARE DANGEROUS. THAT INFORMATION CAN SAVE LIVES.

If park rangers or ski center workers know an avalanche may happen, they can tell people to stay away or use another slope. That warning can keep skiers, snowboarders, and other people from being buried in an avalanche. Good measurements also help officials decide when it's time to make an avalanche. Then they can set off explosions near a dangerous slope to cause the slide when no one is around.

DETERMINING THE RISK

Snow pits are one tool for measuring avalanche risk. A snow pit is a hole dug into snow in a spot where an avalanche may happen. Its walls are often taller than an adult, and it is wide enough for someone to move around in it.

A trained person looks at layers of snow in the sides of the pit. Each layer is a record of one snowfall. The layers may show snowfalls going back to the start of the winter. The person checks each layer. Is it hard packed and stable or unstable and likely to slide? Suppose one deep layer shows sugar snow. That would be a warning that an avalanche could occur.

Some areas have avalanche information centers. These offices keep track of temperatures, wind, and other factors that determine the likelihood of an avalanche. The centers then alert ski areas, parks, and other places if the risk of an avalanche is high.

An expert examines the layers of snow inside a snow pit in Colorado's San Juan Mountains.

AVALANCHE RISK SCALE

Information about avalanche risk also is used to prepare a danger scale. The scale uses different colors to show the risk of an avalanche. Ski centers and parks in avalanche country display these scales during the winter. The scale helps protect people from avalanches.

Different countries may use slightly different colors on their danger scales. The U.S. danger scale uses green, yellow, orange, red, and black.

Green means a low risk of an avalanche. The snow is stable and probably will not slide. People still should use caution. But conditions are safe.

Yellow indicates a moderate risk. Avalanches are unlikely—but still possible on steep slopes. Orange warns of a considerable risk of natural avalanches. People should be more cautious on steeper slopes.

Red means a high risk. People should avoid steep slopes. Red with a black border means an extreme risk. Under these conditions, avalanches are certain to happen. Large, destructive avalanches are possible. People should stay away from steep slopes and areas that could be avalanche runout zones. That might mean leaving cabins or hotels in mountainous areas.

GOLDEN DOG

An avalanche on April 3, 1898, buried hundreds of gold miners on Alaska's Chilkoot Pass. Sixty-five of them died. One amazing survivor was a sled dog named Jack. An old photo album contained a photo of Jack, with this note: "Shorty Fisher's dog Jack who lived eight days under a snow slide." That picture was taken just four weeks after the avalanche. Jack was healthy and pulling Shorty's sled again.

A sign warns skiers of avalanche danger in the Rocky Mountains of Alberta, Canada.

SAVED BY SPIT

People caught in an avalanche often lose their sense of direction. They want to struggle toward the surface. But they can't tell which way is up. If that happens to you, let some spit run out of your mouth. It will run down. But do it before the snow settles, or it won't matter which way is which. You won't be able to move. People will have to dig you out.

AVALANCHE SIZE SCALE

Scientists at the U.S. Forest Service National Avalanche Center often measure the size of avalanches with the destructive force scale. It measures the damage an avalanche could cause, based on the amount of snow that slides. The scale uses the numbers 1 to 5.

A D1 avalanche would involve less than 11 tons (10 metric tons) of snow. It would be relatively harmless. A D4 avalanche, in contrast, would involve 11,025 tons (10,000 metric tons) of snow. That monster avalanche could sweep away railroad trains.

Sometimes scientists use the size-relative to path scale. It compares the actual amount of snow that slid to the amount that could have slipped. An R1 avalanche involves a very small amount of the snow on a mountainside. An R5 avalanche would involve almost all the available snow.

The 1999 avalanche in Austria measured D5.

> ❝ *It doesn't take long to [suffocate].*
> *You get caught in one of those things;*
> *you can't flex a muscle,*
> *let alone breathe.* ❞
>
> —Ian Strathearn, an ambulance worker at an avalanche
> disaster in British Columbia, Canada, in 2003

CODE	AVALANCHE DESTRUCTIVE POWER	TYPICAL MASS	TYPICAL PATH LENGTH
D1	RELATIVELY HARMLESS TO PEOPLE	LESS THAN 11 TONS (10 METRIC TONS)	33 FEET (10 M)
D2	COULD BURY, INJURE, OR KILL A PERSON	110 TONS (100 METRIC TONS)	330 FEET (100 M)
D3	COULD BURY AND DESTROY A CAR, DAMAGE A TRUCK, DESTROY A WOOD FRAME HOUSE, OR BREAK A FEW TREES	1,103 TONS (1,000 METRIC TONS)	3,300 FEET (1,000 M)
D4	COULD DESTROY A RAILWAY CAR, LARGE TRUCK, SEVERAL BUILDINGS, OR A SUBSTANTIAL AMOUNT OF FOREST	11,025 TONS (10,000 METRIC TONS)	6,560 FEET (2,000 M)
D5	COULD GOUGE THE LANDSCAPE; LARGEST SNOW AVALANCHE KNOWN	110,254 TONS (100,000 METRIC TONS)	9,840 FEET (3,000 M)

Snowcapped Mount Huascarán towers over the surrounding area.

1962 and 1970
MOUNT HUASCARÁN, PERU

Ice and snow cover the peak of Mount Huascarán year-round. The mountain is 22,200 feet (6,768 m) high. It towers over several villages in the South American country of Peru.

On January 10, 1962, a huge block of ice broke loose from Mount Huascarán. It shattered into chunks as big as cars as it tumbled toward the village of Ranrahirca.

"I saw it sweep by like a river, carrying away one farmer after another," said Zoila Cristina Angel

"Voices called 'Run! Run!' but I could not run. I could not move. I could not speak. I just looked at that awful thing that came rushing at us like the end of the world."

That avalanche killed four thousand people. It missed the town of Yungay, a larger village nearby. But eight years later, another event caused even more damage.

May 31, 1970, was a warm spring day in Yungay. People were enjoying the beautiful weather. Children played

—**Jorge Flores Garcia, who survived the 1970 avalanche in Yungay**

outside. They were excited about a circus that was in town. Adults went shopping, chatted, and relaxed in the bright sun.

Suddenly a powerful earthquake shook the ground. Jorge Flores Garcia dodged falling bricks and roofs as he tried to keep from falling down. Then he turned toward Mount Huascarán.

"I looked up and saw a cloud of ice dust, like smoke, on the face of Huascarán," he said. The earthquake shook loose a huge sheet of ice on the mountaintop. Jorge knew the giant avalanche was tumbling toward Yungay.

"I ran toward the [hill] to the north of town," Jorge said. He ran to the top. Sweating and out of breath, he turned toward the city. *"Yungay*

A massive landslide buried most of Yungay (aerial view, above) in the 1970 avalanche.

wasn't there," he said. *"A few minutes earlier there was a city and now there was nothing."*

The slab of ice that fell was as wide as seven football fields placed end to end. It was longer than sixteen football fields. As the avalanche hurtled down Mount Huascarán, it gathered dirt, rocks, houses, and trees like a snowball rolling over muddy ground.

The disaster hit Yungay and other villages within four minutes. About 18,000 people died. Thousands of others were injured. It was the most deadly avalanche ever recorded in the world.

The 1970 Yungay avalanche left gigantic piles of debris.

People Helping People

PEOPLE AFFECTED BY AN AVALANCHE OFTEN NEED HELP WITH RESCUE, RELIEF, AND RECOVERY. RESCUE MEANS DIGGING OUT PEOPLE WHO MAY BE BURIED UNDER SNOW, ICE, OR SMASHED BUILDINGS. RELIEF MEANS REDUCING THE SUFFERING OF PEOPLE INVOLVED IN A DISASTER. RECOVERY MEANS HELPING THEM GET THEIR LIVES BACK TO NORMAL.

SEARCH AND RESCUE

After an avalanche, people who are stuck under the snow must be rescued immediately. Snow quickly hardens when it stops moving. Trapped people can't move to get themselves out. They also have a hard time breathing in such a small space. "It's a race against time," said Major Thomas Schoenherr of the Austrian army. He helped rescue victims of a terrible 1999 avalanche.

Most people buried in an avalanche suffocate (die from lack of air) after about 30 minutes. Others may live much longer, especially if they are below the wreckage of a building where there is an airspace.

Bill Zobel was in a café in Edmonton, British Columbia, Canada, in 2004 when an avalanche struck. "It was like a big cannon shot, and I stood up," Zobel remembered. "The next thing I knew I was blown through the wall."

THIRTY-SEVEN DAYS BURIED ALIVE

Three people in Italy may hold the record for staying alive the longest while buried in an avalanche. On March 19, 1775, Maria Anna Rocha was trapped inside a barn when it was covered in 50 feet (15 m) of snow. Her daughter, son, and sister-in-law were with her. On April 24, the snow melted enough to show the roof of the barn. Maria, her daughter, and sister-in-law were still alive. They lived on water from melted snow and milk from goats that were trapped with them.

Rescue workers dig for the bodies of
climbers buried in an avalanche on
December 31, 2005, in northern Slovakia.

He survived for seven hours under 3 feet (0.9 m) of snow by wriggling his head to make a breathing space.

The first help often comes from people who were nearby when the avalanche hit. But finding a buried person can be difficult. The tumbling snow can carry people far from where they were caught in the avalanche.

POLING FOR PEOPLE

Sometimes rescuers can spot a trace of a person. It may be an arm, a leg, or a ski sticking out of the snow. Then they know exactly where to dig.

Rescue workers often have no clues about a victim's location. Then they may use long metal poles to find survivors. The workers stand side by side to form probe lines. They probe (poke) the snow with their poles to feel whether anything is buried underneath. Then they take a step ahead and press again. They stick close together in the line to cover all ground.

AVALANCHE RESCUE BEACONS

People skiing in avalanche country are supposed to carry basic rescue equipment. This equipment usually includes a metal pole for finding buried people, a snow shovel for digging them out, and an avalanche rescue beacon.

A rescue beacon sends and receives a special radio signal. Most are powered by AA batteries and can be strapped to the body. While skiing or hiking, people set the beacon to "send." If someone gets trapped in an avalanche, other people in the group switch their beacons to "receive." Then the survivors' beacons can pick up signals from the victim's. Rescuers use the signal to find the victim.

RESCUE DOGS

Electronic beacons still have not replaced the most famous avalanche rescuers. These rescue experts are trained dogs. Monks living in the Great Saint Bernard Pass in the Swiss Alps began raising these dogs hundreds of years ago. The dogs rescued people who were buried in avalanches or stranded in snowstorms. The dogs became known as Saint Bernards.

Rescuers form a probe line to
search for victims of a 2000
avalanche in Davos, Switzerland.

Saint Bernards are big and strong. Males may be almost 3 feet (0.9 m) high at the shoulders and weigh 200 pounds (91 kilograms). These dogs have thick coats to stay warm in freezing weather.

Saint Bernards have an amazing ability to detect faint odors, sounds, and motion deep below the snow. Years ago, Saint Bernards worked in pairs. The male found and dug up avalanche victims. The female would then cuddle up to the person. She would keep the victim warm while the male ran for help.

Modern rescue dogs travel with their handlers to avalanche sites by helicopter or snowmobile. Many rescue teams use border collies or German shepherds. They are smaller than Saint Bernards and easier to transport.

Well-trained dogs can search an area of snow the size of a football field eight times faster than 20 humans with poles. They do best at finding people who are still alive. When they find a person, they bark, scratch, or point at the snow.

BARRY THE GREAT SAINT

Barry is the world's most famous avalanche dog. This Saint Bernard saved more than 40 lives in the Swiss Alps in the early nineteenth century. For a time, Saint Bernards were called Barry dogs in his honor. After Barry died, he was stuffed and put on display at the Natural History Museum in Berne, Switzerland. He is still there. The Cimetière des Chiens, a pet cemetery near Paris, France, also has a monument (left) to Barry.

Trained dogs can help avalanche search and rescue teams to find victims quickly.

RESCUE AND RELIEF WORKERS

Some ski centers in avalanche danger zones have their own search and rescue teams. These teams are specially trained to rescue victims quickly after an avalanche. Local police, firefighters, and other emergency workers usually also arrive soon after the avalanche strikes. Other rescue and relief teams may fly in from farther away.

"We are going to try and find everyone, dead or alive," said Sergei Shoigu, an emergency worker at the 2002 avalanche in Russia. Recovering dead bodies is important for the families and friends of the victims. It gives them an opportunity to express their sorrow and accept that their loved one is dead.

While rescue and recovery efforts are still going on, other people affected by an avalanche need relief. The avalanche may have destroyed their homes. They need warm clothing, food, water, and a place to stay.

There may be a danger of more avalanches. Many people may have to be evacuated (taken to a safer place) from an avalanche zone. This occurred after a series of terrible avalanches in Europe in 1999. Military bases in Austria, Germany, and Switzerland sent helicopters. They flew more than 2,500 tourists and other people out of the danger zones.

Emergency workers airlifted injured people to hospitals after a February 1999 avalanche in Austria.

Cars lay toppled in the snow following a 1999 avalanche at a ski resort in Austria.

> " *When we arrived . . . we saw*
> **just about everybody was buried.**
> *We just started moving towards signs of life—*
> *a ski glove, digging [and] finding a face,*
> *making sure they're breathing, and moving on.* "

—Abby Watkins, rescue worker at a 2003 avalanche in British Columbia, Canada

RED CROSS AND RED CRESCENT

The International Federation of Red Cross and Red Crescent Societies provide disaster relief all over the world. In the United States and many other countries, Red Cross societies offer food, housing, and other aid to disaster victims. After the 2002 avalanche in North Ossetia, the Russian Red Cross sent 180 family food packages. These 19-pound (8.5 kg) boxes contained enough food to feed a whole family for several days.

Some countries have the Red Crescent instead of the Red Cross. It does the same kind of work. Other relief organizations also pitch in. People who want to help victims of a disaster can donate money to these organizations.

RECOVERY

After rescue and relief, people affected by an avalanche often need help getting their lives back to normal. Cities and villages may have to repair or rebuild roads, bridges, and buildings. People may need new homes. Businesses must get back to work. Recovery might mean permanently moving people to safer areas.

Recovery can take a great deal of money. Government agencies often provide this help. In the United States, the Federal Emergency Management Agency (FEMA) is the main government agency for disaster relief. FEMA provides money to help cities and individuals recover from disaster damage.

After an avalanche disaster,
cleanup may require heavy
machinery and considerable time.

February 9, 2005
KASHMIR, INDIA

An aerial view shows part of the Jammu Region of India. Avalanches devastated the area in early 2005.

In February 2005, the mountainous Kashmir region in northern India received the heaviest snowfalls there in twenty years. About 15 feet (4.6 m) of snow covered many small villages in just several days.

In the village of Waltengoo Nar, Aiysha Shafi had just finished lunch at home on February 19. Suddenly everything went dark. Snow crashed down on her house. Holding her two-year-old son, she was immediately trapped under rubble.

An avalanche had crushed the whole village, killing at least 122 of its 600 residents. Walls of snow 5 to 15 feet (1.5 to 4.6 m) high covered everything. Rescuers dug through the snow to find missing people, but it was a slow process. Shafi recalled, **"I cried, 'Please take me out,' but nobody heard my cries, and I could not move."** She was finally rescued five days later. Her son died within several hours of the avalanche.

Avalanches that day buried villages throughout the region. But because the towns lie in hard-to-reach areas of

An elderly Kashmiri man sits near the debris of destroyed houses.

The Kashmir avalanche destroyed this man's house and killed his children, wife, and mother.

the Himalayas, help from the government and aid organizations did not arrive right away. *"It takes eight hours of walking through heavy snow to reach [those areas],"* explained a police official.

By the time the Indian Army could rescue villagers, many avalanche victims had been trapped for two days. *"Chances of finding survivors are very low,"* reported Lieutenant Colonel VK Batra. Sixty-five-year-old Hanifa Begum beat the odds, however. She survived 50 hours under heavy snow before soldiers pulled her out.

Later that week, the Indian Air Force dropped about three thousand food packets and four hundred blankets from helicopters into disaster areas. Government workers also airlifted thousands of travelers who had been stranded along the highway for six days.

Some residents were angry that they hadn't received help more quickly. *"[The government] didn't consider us worthy of attention,"* said Bashir Ahmed, a school teacher in the village of Viltengnar. His six children all died in the disaster.

Javed Makhdoomi, the inspector general of police, replied that government leaders were only human. They, like everyone, were limited by the snow. *"If you expect magic from us, I am sorry,"* Makhdoomi added.

The disaster destroyed many people's homes and ways of life. Muhammad Shafi, Aiysha's husband, had been a cattle herder, but the avalanche killed his livestock. It also hurt his family. *"All my family members are either dead or injured except me,"* he said. In total, the Kashmir avalanches killed at least 278 people.

Chances of finding survivors are very low.

—Lieutenant Colonel VK Batra of the Indian Army, on the 2005 search and rescue effort in Kashmir

The Future

SCIENTISTS WHO STUDY AVALANCHES LEARNED LESSONS FROM THE TERRIBLE WINTER OF 1999 IN EUROPE. DISASTERS OFTEN TEACH US HOW TO PREDICT AND PREVENT OTHER DISASTERS.

Advance warning of a disaster is very important. When people know that a disaster may happen, they can prepare for it. They may evacuate immediately or get ready to move out of the way.

In the future, scientists hope to forecast avalanches as precisely as they forecast the weather. They want to get answers to questions that can save lives. Exactly where will the avalanche happen? When will it happen? Will the snow tumble in a wild place where nobody lives? Or will it be a killer avalanche that buries a whole town?

AVALANCHE IN A COMPUTER

Scientists studied snowfall and other conditions before the 1999 disasters. They watched snow on mountainsides to see what set off avalanches. They also gathered information about the speed, direction, and damage of the avalanches. That information helps scientists improve their computer models (programs).

Computer models store information about the ingredients for an avalanche. Electronic monitors collect data about snow depth, the kind of snow crystals in each layer, and weather conditions. The computer processes that information. It helps predict whether the snow will slide. It also helps scientists answer those important questions of where? and when? and how big?

Computers at weather information centers
gather and organize weather data. The data
can help scientists predict avalanches.

BETTER MODELS AND COMPUTERS

To make better predictions, scientists need better computer models. As they learn from new avalanches, scientists will improve their models. These computer programs will be more accurate in showing when and where avalanches may happen.

Making and using those models requires advanced supercomputers. These computers are much more powerful than desktop computers. They can solve difficult problems very fast.

AVALANCHE AIR BAGS

In the future, people may have better personal safety devices to help them survive an avalanche. One of these devices may be an inexpensive avalanche air bag. These air bags are already available, but very few people use them because they cost a lot of money.

The air bags protect people in an avalanche by creating an airspace around them. The devices are folded into a special backpack with a container of gas to inflate the bag. A skier caught in an avalanche just pulls a cord. The air bag instantly inflates and expands.

When the avalanche stops, the buried skier lets the air out of the bag. It creates a small space like a cave. Instead of having hard snow packed around the skier's mouth and nose, the skier has room to breathe.

*BANN-*WHAT*-*ERS?

Trees on the side of a mountain act as a natural barrier that can stop an avalanche. When the trees are cut down, an avalanche can whoosh right through the empty space.

In the fourteenth century, rulers of Switzerland made *Bannwalders* (banned woods) laws. The laws helped prevent avalanches by protecting certain mountainside forests. People could "remove nothing, growing or dead, green or withered, lying or standing, small or big, nor remove bark, berries or cones." Sometimes the punishment for cutting these trees was death.

An avalanche class watches a demonstration of an avalanche air bag.

THE AVALUNG

Have you heard of the Aqua Lung? Aqua Lungs supply air for scuba divers to breathe while they are underwater. AvaLungs do much the same for people buried in snow.

The AvaLung straps over a skier's jacket. It has a plastic tube and mouthpiece for breathing. When an avalanche approaches, the skier starts breathing through the mouthpiece.

A filter inside the AvaLung draws air directly from the snow. Even hard-packed snow in an avalanche has plenty of air mixed in. The device also funnels harmful carbon dioxide away from the breathing space while a buried person exhales. By breathing through the AvaLung, a person can stay alive under the snow for more than an hour.

THE AVALANCHE-PROOF PERSON?

No avalanche safety device is perfect. Avalanche air bags, for instance, are expensive. They cost several hundred dollars each. Few people in the United States buy them. In addition, avalanches happen fast. A person caught in an avalanche might not have time to bite onto the AvaLung's mouthpiece. The head-over-heels tumbling in an avalanche may also yank the mouthpiece out.

Even with those safety devices, a person would not be avalanche-proof. Rescue workers still might be unable to locate the buried person. In the future, safety devices may allow victims to breathe for hours while sending out strong signals that lead rescue workers right to them.

DID YOU KNOW?

- A dry slab avalanche can reach speeds of 60 to 80 miles (97 to 129 km) per hour within five seconds.

- Snowmobilers have the highest risk of being killed in an avalanche in the United States.

- In 90 percent of avalanches, the victim or the victim's friends cause the avalanche.

Avalanches can race down slopes at deadly
speeds. Even safety equipment does not
make people avalanche-proof.

AVOIDING AVALANCHE ANXIETY

Avalanches can cause terrible disasters. But don't let the risk of an avalanche spoil your enjoyment of the outdoors during the winter. Avalanches are a danger only for people near steep mountain slopes covered with deep snow. And knowing about avalanches and safety precautions reduces your chances of being hurt by one.

An avalanche, triggered by the local ski patrol, runs down a mountainside in Jackson Hole, Wyoming.

PREPARING FOR AVALANCHES

You can avoid most avalanche danger if you know how to recognize and avoid risky situations and act quickly if an avalanche does happen.

WHEN YOU ARE ENJOYING OUTDOOR ACTIVITIES IN AVALANCHE COUNTRY:

• Read avalanche safety tips provided by ski centers and parks. Pay attention to posted avalanche warnings. Carry an avalanche rescue beacon.

• Never travel alone in backcountry areas. Be sure that a member of your group has experience in avalanche safety.

IF YOU ARE CAUGHT IN AN AVALANCHE:

• Don't try to outrun the snow. Move to the side of the avalanche, out of its path. Try to grab onto a tree, rock, or other sturdy object.

• If you are moving with the snow, make strong swimming motions to stay closer to the surface.

• Keep your mouth closed and teeth clenched. When the snow is settling, cover your mouth and nose with your hands, or with a backpack to provide breathing room.

IF YOU SEE SOMEONE CAUGHT IN AN AVALANCHE:

• Notice where the person goes under, and follow that spot as the snow moves and stops.

• Have emergency rescuers or a nearby adult try to find and dig out the victim.

Timeline

218 B.C. Hannibal crosses the Alps. About 18,000 soldiers, two thousand horses, and several elephants are killed by avalanches.

A.D. 980 Bernard of Menton opens a refuge for travelers in the Alps to protect them from fierce blizzards and avalanches.

1212 The so-called Children's Crusades for capture of the Holy Land of Jerusalem set out across the Alps. Thousands of children die from avalanches and exposure to the extreme temperatures in the mountains.

1476 The Duke of Milan's soldiers attempt to cross the Alps, and 60 soldiers die in an avalanche.

1601 The village of Chèze, in the French Pyrenées mountain range, is destroyed by an avalanche. The disaster kills 107 residents.

1618 An avalanche buries the town of Plurs, Switzerland. Only the residents who are out of town survive.

1695 Monks begin training Saint Bernard dogs and using them as rescue dogs near the Great Saint Bernard Pass in Switzerland *(right)*.

1718 Two avalanches in one day level much of the spa town of Leukerbad, Switzerland, and kill 52 people.

1775 Three people in the Stura Valley area of Italy are rescued after snow trapped them in their barn for 37 days.

1800 Napoleon's troops are struck by an avalanche while crossing the Splugen Pass to Italy.

1898 Sixty-five gold miners die when avalanches bury them on the Chilkoot Pass in Alaska *(left)*.

1910 Snow traps two trains in the Cascade range in Wellington, Washington. Some passengers escape by walking out of the mountains. An avalanche kills the remaining 96 people.

1916 Avalanches in the Tyrol area of Europe kill 18,000 soldiers during World War I. Many more soldiers die in other avalanches throughout the war.

1950–51 Known as the Winter of Terror in the Alps, a series of avalanches kills 265 people.

1954 Blons, Austria, is the site of the worst avalanche in the country's history. A second avalanche, just nine hours after the first, keeps rescuers from the village.

1962 A huge block of ice breaks loose from Mount Huascarán. It buries the village of Ranrahirca, Peru *(below)*, with ice chunks as big as cars.

1969 The world's slowest avalanche occurs on April 12 near Anchorage, Alaska. A wall of snow about 30 feet (9 m) deep slides down at about 2 miles (3.2 km) per hour.

1970 An earthquake causes mud and snow to slide down Mount Huascarán. The town of Yungay, Peru, is buried. About 50 feet (15 m) of rock and snow crashes into the tuberculosis sanatorium in Sallanches, France. It crushes two dormitories and kills 72 nurses and patients.

1979 Five days of snowstorms in the Himalayan foothills of India cause avalanches. The Lahaul Valley is buried in 15 to 20 feet (4 m) of snow.

1992 An avalanche buries the entire city of Gomec, Turkey.

1999 The extreme cold and heavy snows in the Alps of Western Europe cause the worst avalanche season in 50 years.

2002 About 20 million tons (18 million metric tons) of ice fall in Russia's Caucasus Mountains. It tumbles almost 20 miles (32 km) down and onto the surrounding countryside of North Ossetia. Sergei Bodrov, one of Russia's hottest movie stars, is among the 125 people it kills.

2005 In Kamchatka, Russia *(left)*, two reindeer herders are found alive six days after an avalanche buried their tents. In February the Kashmir region of India receives 15 feet (4.6 m) of snowfall within several days. Avalanches kill at least 278 people.

2006 Between December 2005 and March 21, 2006, 53 people die in avalanches in the French Alps, more than any other year on record.

Glossary

avalanche: a large mass of snow or ice that breaks loose from a mountain slope and slides downward

AvaLung: a device that allows people to breathe when buried in the snow

Bannwalders: a German word for trees in an avalanche zone that cannot be cut because they are a natural barrier to avalanches. Switzerland made laws about Bannwalders in the fourteenth century.

computer model: a computer program that uses scientific data to predict when and where an avalanche may happen

depth hoar: a dry, dangerous, deep layer of snow that looks like sugar. Fresh snow falling on top of depth hoar can slide easily and cause an avalanche.

earthquake: a shaking of Earth's surface caused by movements of underground rock

evacuate: to leave a dangerous area and go somewhere safe

loose snow avalanche: an avalanche that occurs when a small amount of snow falls from a point, collecting more snow and fanning out as it slides down

probe line: a line of people who poke long poles into the snow after an avalanche to find buried victims

rescue beacon: a radio device that sends and receives signals to help locate someone buried in an avalanche

Saint Bernard: a breed of dog that is good at rescuing people buried in avalanches

slab avalanche: the most common and deadly kind of avalanche, which happens when a chunk of dry or wet snow slides down

snow crystal: ice that makes up snowflakes. The pattern of flat sides on a snow crystal helps decide how well it will stick to other snow.

stable snow: layers of snow that stick firmly together. They will not slip down and cause an avalanche.

suffocate: to die from lack of air

unstable snow: layers of snow that can easily slip over one another and cause an avalanche

White Death: a term used for avalanches, because they are so dangerous

Places to Visit

Everett, Washington, Public Library
http://www.epls.org/nw/juleen.htm
Photographs from the 1910 Wellington avalanche are housed in the Northwest Room of the library.

Frank Slide Interpretative Center in Alberta, Canada
http://www.cd.gov.ab.ca/enjoying_alberta/museums_historic_sites/site_listings/frank_slide/facility/index.asp
View the damage from the 1903 landslide-avalanche that buried the town.

Glacier National Park in British Columbia, Canada
http://www.britishcolumbia.com/regions/towns/?townID=3496
Travel through the avalanche protection tunnels of Rogers Pass. Check out the visitor center to see models of railway tunnels and films about avalanche control.

Iron Goat Trail near Wellington, Washington
http://www.bcc.ctc.edu/cpsha/irongoat/
Hike and help rebuild the site of an avalanche that took 96 lives when two trains were trapped in the Cascade Mountains.

Klondike Gold Rush National Park in Skagway, Alaska
http://www.nps.gov/klgo
Hike the Chilkoot Pass to see where 65 gold diggers were crushed by avalanches on April 3, 1898.

Source Notes

4   Associated Press, Yuri Bagrov, "Death Toll Up in Russian Avalanche," September 22, 2002, http://www.avalanche-center.org/Incidents/2001-02/20020920-Russia.php (September 2, 2006).

5   John Daniszewski, "Avalanche Wipes Out Village in South Russia," *Los Angeles Times,* September 22, 2002.

5   Ibid.

5   Adrian Humphreys, "Two Time Survivor: Avalanche Expert Describes What It Is Like to Be Buried," *National Post* (Canada), January 21, 2003, A4.

6   Rod Chaytor, "Sledge Hammer Hero of the Alps," *Scottish Daily Record* (Glasgow), February 11, 1999.

8   Candus Thomson, "Uphill Battle Against Avalanches," *Baltimore Sun,* June 4, 2001.

12   Titus Livy, "Hannibal's Route Across the Alps: the Texts," *Livius,* n.d., http://www.livius.org/ha-hd/hannibal/alps_text.html (January 16, 2006).

13   McKay Jenkins, *The White Death: Tragedy and Heroism in an Avalanche* (New York: Random House, 2000), 11.

13   Ibid.

16   Jericho Historical Society, "Wilson A. Bentley— Photographer of Snowflakes," *Snowflakebentley.com,* 2000, http://snowflakebentley.com/index.htm (September 8, 2006).

17   Alison Stenlake, "Avalanche Survivors Tell of Ordeal," *Bristol Evening Post* (England), February 15, 1999, 7.

20–21   JoAnn Roe, *Stevens Pass: The Story of Railroading and Recreation in the North Cascades* (Seattle: Mountaineers, 1995), 88.

21   Ibid., 87.

21   "1910: Trains buried by avalanche," *History.com,* n.d., http://www.history.com/tdih.do?action =tdihArticleCategory&id=359 (October 26, 2006).

23   Thomson, "Uphill Battle Against Avalanches."

26   Joseph Wechsberg, *Avalanche!* (New York: Alfred A. Knopf, 1958), 114.

26 Ibid., 115.

26 Ibid.

26 Ibid.

26 Ibid., 116.

26 Ibid., 114.

27 Ibid., 176.

27 Ibid., 177.

30 Gold Rush Centennial Task Force, State of Alaska, "A Stalwart Dog Survives the Chilkoot Avalanche," *Stories of the Goldrush*, 1999, http://www.library.state.ak.us/goldrush/stories/ave.htm (August 29, 2006).

33 Robert Remington, "Like Swimming Down the Roughest Water: Avalanche Cause Unclear: Survivor Was Buried Except for His Head and His Left Hand," *National Post* (Canada), January 22, 2003, A1.

34 "Carpet of Death," *Time,* January 19, 1962, 38.

35 Associated Press, Kernan Turner, "International News," May 31, 1979.

35 Ibid.

36 Roger Boyes and Susan Bell, "Tyrol Resort Hit by Second Avalanche," *Times* (London), February 25, 1999.

36 David Howell and Jeff Nagel, *Edmonton* (Alberta) *Journal,* January 25, 2004.

42 United Press International, "Five Rescued in Russian Avalanche," *United Press International,* 2006, http://www.upi.com/archive/view.php?archive=1&StoryID=20020924-020733-2345r (January 17, 2006).

43 Robert Remington, "In the Wrong Place at the Wrong Time. Odds of Being Killed by Avalanche Akin to Being Struck by Lightning: Experts," *National Post* (Canada), February 4, 2003, A7.

46 Hari Kumar, "Search Continues for Bodies from Avalanche in Kashmir," *New York Times*, February 28, 2005, http://www.nytimes.com/ (October 20, 2006).

46–47 "Kashmir Avalanche Toll Increases," *BBC News,* February 22, 2005, http://news.bbc.co.uk/ 2/hi/south_asia/4286339.stm (October 20, 2006).

47 Ibid.

47 Altaf Hussain, "A Village Wiped Out by Snow," *BBC News,* February 23, 2005, http://news.bbc.co.uk/2/hi/south_asia/4291121.stm (October 20, 2006).

47 Ibid.

47 Hari Kumar, "Search Continues for Bodies from Avalanche in Kashmir."

50 "Avalanches: Prevention," *Forces of Nature: Think Quest 2000 Team # C003603,* 2000, http://library.thinkquest.org/C003603/english/avalanches/prevention.shtml (August 23, 2006).

Selected Bibliography

Bowers, Vivien. *In the Path of an Avalanche: A True Story.* Vancouver, BC: Greystone Books, 2003.

Burt, Christopher C. *Extreme Weather: A Guide & Record Book.* New York: W. W. Norton & Co., 2004.

Davis, Lee. *Natural Disasters.* New York: Facts on File, 2002.

Engelbert, Phillis. *Dangerous Planet: The Science of Natural Disasters.* Vol. 1. Detroit: U. X. L., 2001.

Fredston, Jill. *Snowstruck: In the Grip of Avalanches.* New York: Harcourt Brace, 2005.

Jenkins, McKay. *The White Death: Tragedy and Heroism in an Avalanche.* New York: Random House, 2000.

Manti-La Sal Avalanche Center. "Avalanche Awareness Tutorial." *LSAFC*. 2003. http://www.avalanche.org/%7Elsafc/TUTORIAL/TUTORIAL.HTM (January 15, 2006).

National Snow and Ice Data Center. "Avalanche Awareness." *nsidc.org*. 2004. http://nsidc.org/snow/avalanche/index.html (January 20, 2006).

Spignesi, Stephen J. *The 100 Greatest Disasters of All Time*. New York: Kensington Publishing Corp, 2002.

"The 10 Worst Snow Disasters in History." *Scientific American.com*. February 16, 2004. http://www.sciam.com/print_version.cfm?articleID=000EC1B8-5DAE-102D-9B7683414B7F0000 (January 15, 2006).

Wechsberg, Joseph. *Avalanche!* New York: Alfred A. Knopf, 1958.

"Wellington Scrapbook: The 1910 Avalanche Disaster." *HistoryLink.org On-Line Encyclopedia of Washington State*. 2002. http://www.historylink.org/wellington/overview.htm (February 1, 2006).

WGBH. "Avalanche!: Elements of a Slide." *NOVA Online*. 1997. http://www.pbs.org/wgbh/nova/avalanche/elements.html (February 10, 2006).

Zeilinga de Boer, Jelle, and Donald Theodore Sanders. *Earthquakes in Human History: The Far-Reaching Effects of Seismic Disruptions*. Princeton, NJ: Princeton University Press, 2005.

Further Resources

BOOKS

Allaby, Michael. *Biomes of the World: Mountains*. Vol. 5. Danbury, CT: Grolier Education, 1999. Read about the causes of avalanches and the measures people have taken to protect themselves.

Barnard, Bryn. *Dangerous Planet: Natural Disasters That Changed History*. New York: Crown Publishers, 2003. This book explores how natural disasters have helped shape the history of the world and how global warming may affect future disasters.

Cosgrove, Brian. *Eyewitness: Weather*. New York: Dorling Kindersley, 2004. Learn all about weather, and see the instruments that have been used to predict and measure weather phenomena.

Creech, Sharon. *Bloomability*. New York: Harper Collins, 1998. In this novel, Lila and Guthrie are swept away in an avalanche while skiing in Italy, and one of them left their transceiver on the school bus!

Kramer, Stephen. *Avalanche*. Minneapolis: Carolrhoda Books, 1992. Beautiful photographs help explain the various types of avalanches and their causes. The book includes avalanche safety tips.

Nash, Jay Robert. *Darkest Hours*. Chicago: Nelson-Hall, 1976. This book tells the stories of historic disasters from ancient civilizations to 1975.

Newson, Lesley. *Devastation: The World's Worst Natural Disasters*. New York: DK Publishing, 1998. Vivid images show how natural disasters affect Earth.

Oliver, Claire. *Natural Disasters: Atlas in the Round*. Philadelphia: Running Press, 2001. Natural disasters are not predictable, but this book explains why certain parts of Earth have the geologic conditions for repeating the same disasters.

Skurzynski, Gloria. *Buried Alive*. Washington, DC: National Geographic, 2003. The Landon kids travel to Alaska with a mysterious acquaintance and are buried by an avalanche. Read how they survive!

WEBSITES AND FILMS

All about Snow
http://nsidc.org/snow/
The National Snow and Ice Data Center site explains all about snow and ice. The information can also be found in *The Snow Booklet* by Nolan J. Doesken and Arthur Judson.

Avalanche!
http://www.nationalgeographic.com/ngkids/0301/
The National Geographic Kids website discusses the formation and speed of avalanches.

Avalanches: Deadly Spectacles of Snow and Ice
http://www.att.com/ehs/safety/avalanches.html
This site is sponsored by AT&T and gives many survival tips for winter weather.

Juneau Avalanche
http://juneaualaska.com/media/video/avalanche/
Watch a streaming video of an avalanche in Juneau, Alaska!

The Palm Sunday Avalanche of 1898
http://www.postalmuseum.si.edu/gold/avalanche.htm
Read tales of avalanches during the Klondike gold rush in Alaska. This website is run by the Postal Museum, part of the Smithsonian Institution in Washington, D.C.

Avalanche. VHS. Bethesda, MD: Discovery Channel, 1997.
This video shows the various types of avalanches and gives tips on remaining safe.

Avalanche: The White Death. DVD and VHS. Washington, DC: National Geographic, 1999.
Learn about the dangers of avalanches from survivor accounts and amazing photography.

Disasters of the Century: In an Instant. Episode no. 12. DVD and VHS. Regina, SK: Partners in Motion, 2003.
This series shows how tragic disasters of the twentieth century have affected communities.

Thunder on the Mountain: Landslides & Avalanches. DVD and VHS. Washington, DC: National Geographic, 1999.
National Geographic brings actual footage of a quiet mountaintop becoming a raging landslide!

Weather Fundamentals: Rain and Snow. DVD and VHS. Wynnewood, PA: Schlessinger Media, 1998.
This video shows students a whirlwind of weather events, including blizzards and avalanches.

Index

Photo Acknowledgments

The images in this book are used with the permission of: © Getty Images, pp. 1, 13, 22, 47 (right); © Alain Frechette/Peter Arnold, Inc., p. 3; © Reuters/CORBIS, p. 4; © Anatoly Maltsev/epa/CORBIS, p. 5; © Tom Murphy/WWI/Peter Arnold, Inc., p. 7; © Papilio/Alamy, p. 9; © P Begnin/Eyevine/ZUMA Press, pp. 10, 55; © Aurora/Getty Images, p. 11; © Bettmann/CORBIS, pp. 12, 27, 56 (bottom); U.S. Geological Survey, p. 15; Courtesy of the National Oceanic and Atmospheric Administration Central Library Photo Collection, p. 16 (all); © CORBIS SYGMA, pp. 17, 32; © Bruce Tremper, pp. 18, 19, 49, 51; Manuscripts, Special Collections, University of Washington Libraries, pp. 20 (A. Curtis, 17481-1), 21 (left -A. Curtis, 17468), (right- A. Curtis, 17461); U. S. Fish and Wildlife Service, p. 23; © Thomas D. Mcavoy/Time Life Pictures/Getty Images, p. 26; © Scott S. Warren/ Aurora/Getty Images, p. 29; P201-154, Alaska State Library, Neal D. Benedict Photograph Collection, p. 30; © Jochen Tack/Peter Arnold, Inc., p. 31; © Gary Brettnacher/SuperStock, p. 33; © Hubertus Kanus/SuperStock, p. 34; © NASA/Time & Life Pictures/Getty Images, p. 35 (top); © Lloyd Cluff/CORBIS, p. 35 (bottom); © REUTERS/STR New, p. 37; © REUTERS/Andy Mettler, p. 39; © Bernard Bisson/CORBIS SYGMA, p. 40; © blickwinkel/Alamy, p. 41; © Thomas Boehm/Tiroler Tageszeitung/CORBIS SYGMA, p. 42; © Hbf/Lechner/ epa/CORBIS, p. 43; © Gregor Schlaeger/VISUM/The Image Works, p. 45; © PIB/TC Malhotra/ZUMA Press, p. 46; © SSHK/TC Malhotra/ZUMA Press, p. 47 (left); Black Diamond Equipment Ltd., p. 52; © Mauritius/ SuperStock, p. 53; © StockShot/Alamy, p. 54; © David Rubinger/Time Life Pictures/Getty Images, p. 56; © Donald Uhrbrock/Time Life Pictures/Getty Images, p. 57 (top); © Ernest Manewal/Visuals Unlimited, p. 57 (bottom).

Diagram p. 15 © Bill Hauser/Independent Picture Service.

Front cover: © S. P. Gillette/CORBIS.
Back cover: Library of Congress (ppmsc 01765).

About the Authors

Michael Woods is a science and medical journalist in Washington, D.C., who has won many national writing awards. Mary B. Woods is a school librarian. Their past books include the eight-volume Ancient Technology series. The Woodses have four children. When not writing, reading, or enjoying their grandchildren, the Woodses travel to gather material for future books.